THE EXECUTIVE'S QUOTATION BOOK

Other quotation books edited by James Charlton

THE EXECUTIVE'S QUOTATION BOOK

(Revised Edition)

Edited by James Charlton

St. Martin's Press   New York

Library of Congress Cataloging-in-Publication Data

The Executive's quotation book : a treasury of wise, witty, cynical,
    and engaging observations about the world of business, law,
    finance, and politics / edited by James Charlton.—Rev. ed.
        p.   cm.
    Rev. ed. of: The Executive's quotation book : a corporate
companion.
    ISBN 0-312-09283-0
    1. Business—Quotations, maxims, etc.   2. Management—
Quotations, maxims, etc.   3. Money—Quotations, maxims, etc.
I. Charlton, James.
PN6084.B87E94   1993
082—dc20   93-7991
                                                        CIP

Second Edition: August 1993

10   9   8   7   6   5   4   3   2   1

INTRODUCTION

I like quotations. There is something about the short form that appeals to me. Maybe it has to do with our diminished attention spans—"quotations are the literary form of the 90s," to quote one wag—but I prefer to think that quotations are a distillation of wit and thought imposed by the brevity of the form. Quotations are not only entertaining to read, but also can be provocative and useful. Nothing shores up an argument or provides an authoritative cap to a conversation like the proper quote; it reflects our education, our erudition. Many times a quote can substitute for a sentiment or opinion that we ourselves would dare not utter. But put quotation marks around it and attribute it to Twain or Forbes and you can get away unscathed.

"Every quotation contributes something to the stability and enlargement of the langugage," Samuel Johnson generously opined, and I agree. *Good* quotes—those that make their way into the consciousness of a people— seem almost to spring up on their own. Oftentimes they are attributed to individuals who never said them, or who said them in quite a different form or context. We take them up and edit, shape, and polish them to fit our needs. Whether Leo Durocher ever said, "Nice guys finish last," when referring to the Dodgers, doesn't matter. The phrase was too good, too useful in a variety of situations, to let go unrepeated.

The financial and business worlds are particularly rich fields for quotations, since they are areas that touch all our lives. Opinions, reflections, regrets, gloating, admonishments, warnings, and advice abound. Some are pompous, while others are unassuming and reflect a very noncorporate view of the world. Many of the wittiest come not just from the credentialed humorists such as Mark Twain, Will Rogers, and Oscar Wilde, but also from unlikely wordsmiths like Henry Ford, J. Paul Getty, and Warren Buffett, all of whom are marvelously funny on the subject of business.

When we gathered the entries for the first edition of *The Executive's Quotation Book* more than ten years ago, we resisted the suggestion to include every opinion and statement ever uttered about business, work, getting ahead, et cetera. I find those books eye-glazingly dull. Although this revision is greatly edited and expanded by more than fifty percent, the book is still not meant to be all-inclusive, even in the subject areas we've staked out for it. We have tried to catalog only quotations that are insightful, amusing, or surprising to anyone reading for amusement or to glean a choice turn of phrase for a speech. We have kept the adages, maxims, and anonymous quotes to a bare minimum and tried to list phrases that were penned or uttered by individuals with whom any literate business person ought to be acquainted. For that reason, there is almost no listing of source, date, or corporate affiliation.

There are a number of more encyclopedic sources of quotations such as *Bartlett's Familiar Quotations*, *The Macmillan Dictionary of Quotations*, and the *Oxford Book of Quotations* that I acknowledge, respect, and recommend for everyone's library. To those books I leave subject lists, key words, first-line indexes and such. The quotations in *The Executive's Quotation Book* are arranged loosely according to subject matter, and there is an index of names to help you find your way. But the real test of a book of quotations like this is enjoyment, and to that end I hope this satisfies.

Business? It's quite simple—it's other people's money.
ALEXANDRE DUMAS

Business is the oldest of the arts, the newest of professions.
LAURENCE LOWELL, *first president of the Harvard Business School*

Business has only two basic functions—marketing and innovation.
PETER DRUCKER

Business is a combination of war and sport.
ANDRÉ MAUROIS

What recommends commerce to me is its enterprise and bravery. It does not clasp its hands and pray to Jupiter.
HENRY DAVID THOREAU

It very seldom happens to a man that his business is his pleasure.
SAMUEL JOHNSON

Business is never so healthy as when, like a chicken, it must do a certain amount of scratching for what it gets.
HENRY FORD

The secret in business is to know something that nobody else knows.
ARISTOTLE ONASSIS

I don't know anything about business, but I know everything about my own business.
CHARLES AZNAVOUR

My own business bores me to death. I prefer other people's.
OSCAR WILDE

Few people do business well who do nothing else.
EARL OF CHESTERFIELD

A man is known by the company he organizes.
AMBROSE BIERCE

A trust is known by the companies it keeps.
ELLIS O. JONES

A businessman is a hybrid of a dancer and a calculator.
PAUL VALÉRY

In business, the competition will bite you if you keep running; if you stand still, they will swallow you.
WILLIAM KNUDSEN

I have always believed that it's important to show a new look periodically. Predictability can lead to failure.

T. BOONE PICKENS

You can't sit on the lid of progress. If you do, you will be blown to pieces.

HENRY KAISER

Business more than any other occupation is a continual dealing with the future: It is a continual calculation, an instinctive exercise in foresight.

HENRY R. LUCE

Never rest on your oars. If you do, the whole company starts sinking.

LEE IACOCCA

A fellow doesn't last long on what he has done. He's got to keep on delivering as he goes along.

CARL HUBBELL

The most successful businessman is the man who holds onto the old just as long as it is good, and grabs the new just as soon as it is better.

ROBERT P. VANDERPOEL

If you want to succeed you should strike out on new paths rather than travel the worn paths of accepted success.

JOHN D. ROCKEFELLER, JR.

Markets change, tastes change, so the companies and the individuals who choose to compete in those markets must change.

DR. AN WANG

When it comes time to hang the capitalists they will compete with each other to sell us the rope at a lower price.

LENIN

Forget your opponents; always play against par.

SAM SNEAD

The trouble in American life today, in business as well as sports, is that too many people are afraid of competition. The result is that, in some circles, people have come to sneer at success, if it costs hard work and training and sacrifice.

KNUTE ROCKNE

One of my lawyers told me to read the sports section first every morning. It talks of mankind's successes, while other parts talk about mankind's problems or failures.

MICHAEL MILKEN

Nobody talks more of free enterprise and competition and of the best man winning than the man who inherited his father's store or farm.

C. WRIGHT MILLS

4

Sometimes by losing a battle you find a new way to win the war.

DONALD TRUMP

Whoever said, "It's not whether you win or lose that counts," probably lost.

MARTINA NAVRATILOVA

A man is not finished when he is defeated. He is finished when he quits.

RICHARD NIXON

In a boxing match, you can lose the first fourteen rounds. All you have to do is nail your opponent in the last ten seconds of the fifteenth round and you're the world's heavyweight champion.

H. ROSS PEROT

Nothing is quite honest that is not commercial, but not everything commercial is honest.

ROBERT FROST

Men of business must not break their word twice.

THOMAS FULLER

Nothing is illegal if a hundred businessmen decide to do it, and that's true anywhere in the world.

ANDREW YOUNG

It is no secret that organized crime in America takes in over forty billion dollars a year. This is quite a profitable sum, especially when one considers that the Mafia spends very little for office supplies.

WOODY ALLEN

Ethics stay in the preface of the average business science book.

PETER DRUCKER

It is a matter of having principle. It's easy to have principles when you're rich. The important thing is to have principles when you're poor.

RAY KROC

Eats first, morals after.

BERTOLT BRECHT

If it ever came to a choice between compromising my moral principles and the performance of my duties, I know I'd go with my moral principles.

GENERAL NORMAN SCHWARTZKOPF

I ran the wrong kind of business, but I did it with integrity.

SYDNEY BIDDLE BARROWS, *The Mayflower Madam*

The CEO who misleads others in public may eventually mislead himself in private.
WARREN BUFFETT

It is a socialist idea that making profits is a vice; I consider the real vice is making losses.
WINSTON CHURCHILL

The worst crime against working people is a company which fails to operate at a profit.
SAMUEL L. GOMPERS

Business without profit is not business anymore than a pickle is candy.
CHARLES F. ABBOTT

A business that makes nothing but money is a poor business.
HENRY FORD

Volume times zero isn't too healthy.
LEE IACOCCA

Rule number 1: Never lose money.
Rule number 2: Never forget rule no. 1.
WARREN BUFFETT

There is something sick about a person whose only interest is money. And the same can be said, I think, for the company whose sole goal is profit.

RICHARD HAAYAN

If a man goes into business with only the idea of making money, chances are he won't.

JOYCE CLYDE HALL

In the business world, everyone is paid in two coins: cash and experience. Take the experience first; the cash will come later.

HAROLD GENEEN

That's the American way. If little kids don't aspire to make money like I did, what the hell good is this country?

LEE IACOCCA

When I was seventeen or so,
I scoffed at money grubbers.
I had a cold contempt for dough,
and I wouldn't wear my rubbers.

OGDEN NASH

Poverty is uncomfortable; but nine times out of ten the best thing that can happen to a young man is to be tossed overboard and compelled to sink or swim.

JAMES A. GARFIELD

Develop your eccentricities while you are young. That way, when you get old, people won't think you're going gaga.

DAVID OGILVY

Take your hats off to the past, but take your coats off to the future.

CLARE BOOTHE LUCE

Don't learn the tricks of the trade—learn the trade.

JAMES CHARLTON

A résumé is a balance sheet without liabilities.

ROBERT HALF

When you're green you grow. When you're ripe, you rot.

RAY KROC

The way for a young man to rise is to improve himself every way he can, never suspecting that anybody wishes to hinder him.

ABRAHAM LINCOLN

Success in business requires training and discipline and hard work. But if you're not frightened by these things, the opportunities are just as great today as they ever were.

DAVID ROCKEFELLER

Don't be misled into believing that somehow the world owes you a living. The boy who believes that his parents, or the government, or anyone else owes him his livelihood and that he can collect it without labor will wake up one day and find himself working for another boy who did not have that belief and, therefore, earned the right to have others work for him.

DAVID SARNOFF

Ability has nothing to do with opportunity.

NAPOLEON BONAPARTE

Your attitude, not your aptitude, will determine your altitude.

ZIG ZIGLAR

In the game of life it's a good idea to have a few early losses, which relieves you of the pressure of trying to maintain an undefeated season.

BILL VAUGHAN

To keep an organization young and fit, don't hire anyone until everybody's so overworked they'll be glad to see the newcomer no matter where he sits.

ROBERT TOWNSEND

Young men are fitter to invent than to judge; fitter for execution than for counsel; and fitter for new projects than for settled business.

FRANCIS BACON

Old men are always advising young men to save money. That is bad advice. Don't save every nickel. Invest in yourself. I never saved a dollar until I was forty years old.

HENRY FORD

Money, which represents the prose of life, and is hardly spoken of in parlors without apology, is, in its effects and laws, as beautiful as roses.

RALPH WALDO EMERSON

You can be as romantic as you please about love, Hector; but you mustn't be romantic about money.

GEORGE BERNARD SHAW, *Heartbreak House*

Money, it turned out, was exactly like sex; you thought of nothing else if you didn't have it and thought of other things if you did.

JAMES BALDWIN

Money is like manure. If you spread it around, it does a lot of good, but if you pile it up in one place, it stinks like hell.

CLINT MURCHISON

Money brings a certain happiness, but after a certain point, it just brings more money.
    NEIL SIMON

The entire essence of America is the hope to first make money—then make money with money—then make lots of money with lots of money.
    PAUL ERDMAN

Money doesn't change men, it merely unmasks them. If a man is naturally selfish or arrogant or greedy, the money brings that out, that's all.
    HENRY FORD

I don't like money actually, but it quiets my nerves.
    JOE LOUIS

It is true that money attracts, but much money repels.
    CYNTHIA OZICK

I've been in trouble all my life; I've done the most unutterable rubbish, all because of money. I didn't need it . . . the lure of the zeros was simply too great.
    RICHARD BURTON

Make money and the whole world will conspire to call you a gentleman.
    MARK TWAIN

So you think that money is the root of all evil. Have you ever asked what is the root of money?

AYN RAND

Not to be covetous is money in your purse; not to be eager to buy is income.

CICERO

The covetous man never has money; the prodigal will have none shortly.

BEN JONSON

Who needs money when you're funny.

RANDY NEWMAN

The petty economics of the rich are just as amazing as the silly extravagances of the poor.

WILLIAM FEATHER

I would rather have my people laugh at my economics than weep for my extravagance.

OSCAR II OF SWEDEN

Money is a terrible master, but an excellent servant.

P. T. BARNUM

The value of money is that with it we can tell any man to go to the devil. It is the sixth sense, which enables you to enjoy the other five.

W. SOMERSET MAUGHAM

I'd love to sell out completely. It's just that no one's willing to buy.

JOHN WATERS

I'd like to have money. And I'd like to be a good writer. These two can come together, and I hope they will, but if that's too adorable, I'd rather have money.

DOROTHY PARKER

There is no doubt about it, there is no pleasure like it, the sudden splendid spending of money and we spent it.

GERTRUDE STEIN

I believe in the dollar. Everything I earn, I spend!

JOAN CRAWFORD

I have enough money to last the rest of my life, unless I buy something.

JACKIE MASON

Actually, I have no regard for money. Aside from its purchasing power, it's completely useless as far as I'm concerned.

ALFRED HITCHCOCK

The only people who claim that money is not important are people who have enough money so that they are relieved of the ugly burden of thinking about it.

JOYCE CAROL OATES

Some people say that the power was green power. I must say that without green power you cannot make it, but you need love power to handle green power.

LITTLE RICHARD

It's important to recognize I didn't start out on a level of faith working with millions of dollars. . . . I started out by believing God for a newer car than the one I was driving. I started out believing God for a nicer apartment than I had. Then I moved up.

JIM BAKKER

If only God would give me some clear sign! Like making a deposit in my name in a Swiss bank account.

WOODY ALLEN

Money may be the husk of may things, but not the kernel. It brings you food, but not appetite; medicine, but not health; acquaintances, but not friends; servants, but not faithfulness; days of joy, but not peace or happiness.

HENRIK IBSEN

There are three great friends: an old wife, an old dog, and ready money.

BENJAMIN FRANKLIN

Money doesn't buy friends, but it allows a better class of enemies.

LORD MANCROFT

Money and time are the heaviest burdens of life, and the unhappiest of all mortals are those who have more of either than they know what to do.

SAMUEL JOHNSON

Money talks. The more money the louder it talks.

ARNOLD ROTHSTEIN

That money talks
I'll not deny,
I heard it once;
It said, "Good-bye."

RICHARD ARMOUR

My boy . . . always try to rub up against money, for if you rub up against money long enough, some of it may rub off on you.

DAMON RUNYON

Too much of a good thing can be wonderful.
MAE WEST

I think greed is healthy. You can be greedy and still feel good about yourself.
IVAN BOESKY

I have one basic drive on my side they can't defeat—greed.
FRANK ZAPPA

Everything in the world may be endured except continued prosperity.
GOETHE

It seems to be a law of American life that whatever enriches us anywhere except in the wallet inevitably becomes uneconomic.
RUSSELL BAKER

Surplus wealth is a sacred trust which its possessor is bound to administer in his lifetime for the good of the community.
ANDREW CARNEGIE

Being very rich, as far as I am concerned, is having a margin. The margin is being able to give.
MAY SARTON

Prosperity is only an instrument to be used, not a deity to be worshipped.

CALVIN COOLIDGE

Make money your God, and it will plague you like the devil.

HENRY FIELDING

The highest use of capital is not to make money, but to make money do more for the betterment of life.

HENRY FORD

Try not to become a man of success but rather try to become a man of value.

ALBERT EINSTEIN

There is nothing wrong with men possessing riches but the wrong comes when riches possess men.

BILLY GRAHAM

No one would remember the Good Samaritan if he'd only had good intentions. He had money as well.

MARGARET THATCHER

The more money an American accumulates, the less interesting he becomes.

GORE VIDAL

A feast is made for laughter,
And wine maketh merry,
But money answereth all things.
Ecclesiastes 10:19

The man who damns his money has obtained it dishonorably; the man who respects it has earned it.
AYN RAND

I don't want to make money. I just want to be wonderful.
MARILYN MONROE

I don't want to be a star, I want to be a millionaire.
KINKY FRIEDMAN

The much maligned idle rich have received a bad rap: They have maintained or increased their wealth while many of the energetic rich—aggressive real estate operators, corporate acquirers, oil drillers, etc.—have their fortunes disappear.
WARREN BUFFETT

You know, Ernest, the rich are different from us.
F. SCOTT FITZGERALD

Yes, I know. They have more money.
ERNEST HEMINGWAY

As a general rule, nobody has money who ought to have it.

BENJAMIN DISRAELI

Sudden money is going from zero to two hundred dollars a week. The rest doesn't count.

NEIL SIMON

A man who has a million dollars is as well off as if he were rich.

JOHN JACOB ASTOR

What I call loaded I'm not. What other people called loaded I am.

ZSA ZSA GABOR

I can buy and sell any of those people who are always criticizing me.

PIA ZADORA

If you would know what the Lord God thinks of money, you have only to look at those to whom he gives it.

MAURICE BARING

To suppose, as we all suppose, that we could be rich and not behave as the rich behave, is like supposing that we could drink all day and keep absolutely sober.

LOGAN PEARSALL SMITH

What's the sense in getting rich if you just stare at the ticker tape all day?

WARREN BUFFETT

With all the unrest in the world, I don't think anybody should have a yacht that sleeps more than twelve.

TONY CURTIS, *Some Like It Hot*

I'd like to be rich enough to throw soap away after the letters are worn off.

ANDY ROONEY

If you can count your money, you don't have a billion dollars.

J. PAUL GETTY

People who know how much they're worth aren't usually worth that much.

NELSON BUNKER HUNT

To turn $100 into a $110 is work. To turn $100 million into $110 million is inevitable.

EDGAR BRONFMAN

The only way to keep score in business is to add up how much money you make.

HARRY HELMSLEY

Money is a stupid measure of achievement, but unfortunately it is the only universal measure we have.

CHARLES STEINMETZ

Thieves respect property. They merely wish the property to become their property that they may more perfectly respect it.

G. K. CHESTERTON

Buy land, they're not making it anymore.

MARK TWAIN

When the white man came, we had the land and they had the Bibles. Now they have the land and we have the Bibles.

CHIEF DAN GEORGE

Government has no other end but the preservation of property.

JOHN LOCKE

Property is the fruit of labor; property is desirable; it is a positive good in the world. That some should be rich shows that others may become rich, and, hence, is just another encouragement to industry and enterprise.

ABRAHAM LINCOLN

Most people seek after what they do not possess and are enslaved by the very things they want to acquire.
ANWAR SADAT

Possession diminishes perception of value, immediately.
JOHN UPDIKE

It is preoccupation with possession, more than anything else, that prevents men from living freely and nobly.
BERTRAND RUSSELL

Possessions, outward success, publicity, luxury—to me these have always been contemptible. I believe that a simple and unassuming manner of life is best for everyone, best both for the body and the mind.
ALBERT EINSTEIN

Neither great poverty nor great riches will hear reason.
HENRY FIELDING

Poor people know poor people and rich people know rich people. It is one of the few things La Rochefoucauld did not say, but then La Rochefoucauld never lived in the Bronx.
MOSS HART

The trouble with being poor is that it takes up all your time.
WILLEM DE KOONING

There were times my pants were so thin that I could sit on a dime and tell if it were heads or tails.
SPENCER TRACY

Almost all the noblest things that have been achieved in the world have been achieved by poor men, poor scholars, poor professional men, poets, and men of genius. A certain staidness and sobriety, a certain moderation and restraint, a certain pressure of circumstances are good for men. His body was not made for luxuries. It sickens, sinks, and dies under them.
HENRY DAVID THOREAU

I'd like to live like a poor man with lots of money.
PABLO PICASSO

I never wanted to be a millionaire. I just wanted to live like one.
WALTER HAGEN

I am not rich. I am a poor man with money, which is not the same thing.
GABRIEL GARCIA MARQUEZ

Mamma may have
Papa may have
But God bless the child that's got his own.
That's got his own.
BILLIE HOLIDAY

Saving is a very fine thing, especially when your parents have done it for you.

WINSTON CHURCHILL

Money is always there but the pockets change; it is not in the same pockets after a change, and that is all there is to say about money.

GERTRUDE STEIN

When a fellow says, "It ain't the money but the principle of the thing," it's the money.

FRANK MCKINNEY "KIN" HUBBARD

I've been rich and I've been poor, and believe me, rich is better.

JOE E. LEWIS

If you were poor enough, long enough, you always feel your wealth could be taken from you.

MARK GOODSON

I've never been poor, only broke. Being poor is a frame of mind. Being broke is only a temporary situation.

MIKE TODD

Solvency is entirely a matter of temperament and not of income.

LOGAN PEARSALL SMITH

"WHAT A FALL WAS THERE, MY COUNTRYMEN!"

I'm living so far beyond my income that we might be said to be living apart.

SAKI (H. H. MUNRO)

My problem lies in reconciling my gross habits with my net income.

ERROL FLYNN

It may be that Chrysler was just a little ahead of its time. It went bankrupt quicker than most everybody else.

LEE IACOCCA

Capitalism without bankruptcy is like Christianity without hell.

FRANK BORMAN

Creditors have better memories than debtors.

BENJAMIN FRANKLIN

There are occasions when it is undoubtedly better to incur loss than to make gain.

PLAUTUS

Don't let your mouth write no check your tail can't cash.

BO DIDDLEY

In God we trust, all others pay cash.
Sign used in retail stores during the Depression

No man's credit is as good as his money.
E. W. HOWE

Money is the poor people's credit card.
MARSHALL McLUHAN

Expenditure rises to meet income. Individual expenditure not only rises to meet income but tends to surpass it.
C. NORTHCOTE PARKINSON, *The Law of Profits*

No man can be conservative until he has something to lose.
JAMES WARBURG

I have tried to become conservative. In 1958 I resolved to be simply a piano player. That was the year I lost $800,000.
LIBERACE

Finance is the art of passing currency from hand to hand until it finally disappears.
ROBERT SARNOFF

Finance is the art or science of managing revenues and resources for the best advantage of the manager.

AMBROSE BIERCE

Money is to be respected; one of the worst things you can do is handle another person's money without respect for how it was earned.

T. BOONE PICKENS

Where large sums of money are concerned, it is advisable to trust nobody.

AGATHA CHRISTIE

With an evening coat and a white tie, even a stockbroker can gain a reputation for being civilized.

OSCAR WILDE

The bulls make money.
The bears make money.
But the pigs get slaughtered.
    Wall Street axiom

October is one of the peculiarly dangerous months to speculate in stocks. The others are July, January, September, April, November, May, March, June, December, August, and February.

MARK TWAIN

Wall Street. A thoroughfare that begins in a graveyard and ends in a river.

ANONYMOUS

There is no more mean, stupid, pitiful, selfish, ungrateful animal than the stock-speculating public. It is the greatest of cowards, for it is afraid of itself.

WILLIAM HAZLITT

Do you know the only thing that gives me pleasure? It's seeing my dividends roll in.

JOHN D. ROCKEFELLER, JR.

Never invest your money in anything that eats or needs repainting.

BILLY ROSE

There is nothing so disastrous as a rational investment policy in an irrational world.

JOHN MAYNARD KEYNES

My central principle of investment is to go contrary to general opinion, on the grounds that, if everyone agreed to its merits, the investment is inevitably too dear and therefore unattractive.

JOHN MAYNARD KEYNES

Buy when everyone is selling. And hold until everyone is buying.

J. PAUL GETTY

Fools rush in where angels fear to trade.

RAY DEVOE

We believe that according the name "investors" to institutions that trade actively is like calling someone who repeatedly engages in one-night stands a romantic.

WARREN BUFFETT

What makes a good trader more than anything is the willingness to take losses.

LEW GLUCKSMAN

The wise man understands equity; the small man understands only profits.

CONFUCIUS

There are only two times in a man's life when he should not speculate; when he can't afford it, and when he can.

MARK TWAIN

There is scarcely an instance of a man who has made a fortune by speculation and kept it.

ANDREW CARNEGIE

There is no moral difference between gambling at cards or in lotteries or on the race track and gambling in the stock market. One method is just as pernicious to the body politic as the other kind, and in degree the evil worked is far greater.

    THEODORE ROOSEVELT

As time goes on, I get more and more convinced that the right method in investment is to put fairly large sums into enterprises which one thinks one knows something about and in the management of which one thoroughly believes.

    JOHN MAYNARD KEYNES

Gambling with cards or dice, or stocks, is all one thing; it is getting money without giving an equivalent for it.

    HENRY WARD BEECHER

If you bet on a horse, that's gambling. If you bet you can make three spades, that's entertainment. If you bet cotton will go up three points, that's business. See the difference?

    WILLIAM "BLACKIE" SHERROD

One of these days in your travels a guy is going to come up to you and show you a nice brand-new deck of cards on which the seal is not yet broken, and this guy is going to offer to bet you that he can make the jack of spades jump out of the deck and squirt cider in your ear. But, son, do not bet this man, for as sure as you stand there, you are going to wind up with an earful of cider.

DAMON RUNYON

There were a few hustlers who depended upon suckers for survival. And there were some who were too wise to hustle, who only wanted enough money to be able to afford to be a sucker.

DUKE ELLINGTON

When you are skinning your customers, you should leave some skin on to grow so that you can skin them again.

NIKITA KHRUSHCHEV

Neither a borrower nor a lender be;
For loan oft loses both itself and friend,
And borrowing dulls the edge of husbandry.

WILLIAM SHAKESPEARE

It is better to give than to lend, and it costs about the same.

SIR PHILIP GIBBS

Let us all be happy and live within our means, even if we have to borrow the money to do it with.

C. F. BROWNE (ARTEMUS WARD, *pseudonym*)

I get by with a little help from my friends.
JOHN LENNON & PAUL MCCARTNEY

Credit buying is much like being drunk. The buzz happens immediately and gives you a lift. . . . The hangover comes the day after.
DR. JOYCE BROTHERS

Economy is in itself a source of great revenue.
SENECA

The human species, according to the best theory and form of it, is composed of two distinct races, the men who borrow, and the men who lend.
CHARLES LAMB

There have been three great inventions since the beginning of time: fire, the wheel, and central banking.
WILL ROGERS

Banking establishments are more dangerous than standing armies.
THOMAS JEFFERSON

Banking may well be a career from which no man really recovers.
JOHN KENNETH GALBRAITH

A banker is a fellow who lends you his umbrella when the sun is shining and wants it back the minute it begins to rain.

MARK TWAIN

If you would know the value of money, go and try to borrow some.

BENJAMIN FRANKLIN

When a man is going to try and borrow money, it is wise to look prosperous.

BENJAMIN DISRAELI

One rule which woe betides the banker who fails to heed it.
Never lend any money to anybody unless they don't need it.

OGDEN NASH

Why rob banks? That's where the money is.

WILLIE SUTTON

What is robbing a bank compared with founding a bank.

BERTOLT BRECHT

If you owe a bank enough money you own it.

ANONYMOUS

If you don't have some bad loans you are not in business.
PAUL VOLCKER

The banks couldn't afford me. That's why I had to be in business for myself.
SAMUEL GOLDWYN

It's so American to start one's own business.
ANNE McDONNELL FORD

When I was young, I worked for a capitalist twelve hours a day and I was always tired. Now I work for myself twenty hours a day and I never get tired.
NIKITA KHRUSHCHEV

Chop your own wood, and it will warm you twice.
HENRY FORD

In soloing—as in other activities—it is far easier to start something than it is to finish it.
AMELIA EARHART

An eminent lawyer cannot be a dishonest man. Tell me a man is dishonest and I will answer he is no lawyer. He cannot be, because he is careless and reckless of justice; the law is not in his heart, is not the standard and rule of his conduct.
DANIEL WEBSTER

I don't want a lawyer to tell me what I cannot do; I hire him to tell me how to do what I want to do.
J. P. MORGAN

The first thing we do, let's kill all the lawyers.
WILLIAM SHAKESPEARE

Necessity has no law; I know some attorneys of the same.
BENJAMIN FRANKLIN

I think we may class the lawyer in the natural history of monsters.
JOHN KEATS

An oral contract isn't worth the paper it's written on.
SAMUEL GOLDWYN

He is no lawyer who cannot take two sides.
CHARLES LAMB

It is the trade of lawyers to question everything, yield nothing, and to talk by the hour.
THOMAS JEFFERSON

Lawyers have been known to wrest from reluctant juries triumphant verdicts of acquittal for their clients, even

when those clients, as often happens, were clearly and
unmistakably innocent.

OSCAR WILDE

Lawyers make a living trying to figure out what other
lawyers have written.

WILL ROGERS

Whether you're an honest man or whether you're a thief
depends on whose solicitor has given me a brief.

W. S. GILBERT, *Utopia Limited*

Discourage litigation. Persuade your neighbor to com-
promise whenever you can. As a peacemaker the lawyer
has a superior opportunity of being a good man. There
will still be business enough.

ABRAHAM LINCOLN

Luck is the residue of design.

BRANCH RICKEY

Luck is the by-product of busting your ass.

DON SUTTON

I am a great believer in luck, and I find the harder I work
the more I have of it.

STEPHEN LEACOCK

Work is love made visible.
KAHLIL GIBRAN

Work is the only rent you pay for the room you occupy on earth.
ELIZABETH II

We work to become, not to acquire.
ELBERT HUBBARD

The labourer is worthy of his hire.
Luke 10:7

Work is much more fun than fun.
NOEL COWARD

(1) Out of clutter find simplicity
(2) From discord find harmony
(3) In the middle of difficulty lies opportunity.
ALBERT EINSTEIN, *his three rules of work*

The reason a lot of people do not recognize opportunity is because it usually goes around wearing overalls looking like hard work.
THOMAS EDISON

Ninety percent of the work done in this country is by people who don't feel well.
THEODORE ROOSEVELT

Showing up is eighty percent of life.
WOODY ALLEN

The better work men do is always done under stress and at great personal cost.
WILLIAM CARLOS WILLIAMS

My father taught me to work hard. He did not teach me to love it. I never did like to work and I don't deny it. I'd rather read, tell stories, crack jokes, talk, laugh—anything but work.
ABRAHAM LINCOLN

Never confuse motion for action.
ERNEST HEMINGWAY

Don't tell me how hard you work. Tell me how much you get done.
JAMES LING

When your work speaks for itself, don't interrupt.
HENRY KAISER

As others toil for me, I must toil for others.
Ecclesiastes 2:20

If he works for you, you work for him.
Japanese proverb

The man who is employed for wages is as much a businessman as his employer.

WILLIAM JENNINGS BRYAN

It is not the employer who pays wages—he only handles the money. It is the product that pays wages.

HENRY FORD

It's not what you pay a man but what he costs you that counts.

WILL ROGERS

There are two things needed in these days; first, for rich men to find out how poor men live; and, second, for poor men to know how rich men work.

E. ATKINSON

If hard work were such a wonderful thing, surely the rich would have kept it all to themselves.

LANE KIRKLAND

If you want a thing done, go—if not, send.

BEN FRANKLIN

It takes less time to do a thing right than to explain why you did it wrong.

HENRY WADSWORTH LONGFELLOW

44

A man would do nothing if he waited until he could do it so well that no one could find fault.

JOHN HENRY CARDINAL NEWMAN

People forget how fast you did a job—but they remember how well you did it.

HOWARD W. NEWTON

I never got a (high school) degree, and I've only worked half days my entire career. I guess my advice to you is to do the same. Work half days every day. And it doesn't matter which half. The first twelve hours or the second twelve hours.

KEMMONS WILSON

There are no traffic jams when you go the extra mile.

ANONYMOUS

It never fails: Everybody who really makes it does it by busting his ass.

ALAN ARKIN

If you think you can, you can. If you think you can't, you're right.

MARY KAY ASH

No ethic is as ethical as the work ethic.

JOHN KENNETH GALBRAITH

The world is an oyster but you don't crack it open on a mattress.

ARTHUR MILLER

The first man gets the oyster, the second man gets the shell.

ANDREW CARNEGIE

The world is full of willing people; some willing to work, the rest willing to let them.

ROBERT FROST

If you don't want to work, you have to earn enough money so that you won't have to work.

OGDEN NASH

Robinson Crusoe started the forty-hour week. He had all his work done by Friday.

LEOPOLD FECHTNER

I worked for charity all my life and now it's kind of fun to work for money.

CHARLOTTE FORD

I've always worried about people who are willing to work for nothing. Sometimes that's all you get from them, nothing.

SAM ERVIN

Like every man of sense and good feeling, I abominate work.

ALDOUS HUXLEY

I do not like work even when another person does it.

MARK TWAIN

We work not only to produce but to give value to time.

EUGENE DELACROIX

I have succeeded in getting my actual work down to thirty minutes a day. That leaves me eighteen hours for engineering.

CHARLES STEINMETZ

One has to look out for engineers—they begin with sewing machines and end up with the atomic bomb.

MARCEL PAGNOL

Nothing is really work unless you would rather be doing something else.

SIR JAMES BARRIE

I get satisfaction of three kinds. One is creating something, one is being paid for it, and one is the feeling that I haven't just been sitting on my ass all afternoon.

WILLIAM F. BUCKLEY

What we call "creative work" ought not to be called work at all, because it isn't. . . . I imagine that Thomas Edison never did a day's work in his last fifty years.
STEPHEN LEACOCK

Results? Why, man, I have gotten a lot of results. I know 50,000 things that won't work.
THOMAS EDISON

People who work sitting down get paid more than people who work standing up.
OGDEN NASH

Clearly the most unfortunate people are those who must do the same thing over and over again, every minute, or perhaps twenty to the minute. They deserve the shortest hours and the highest pay.
JOHN KENNETH GALBRAITH

The difference between a job and a career is the difference between forty and sixty hours a week.
ROBERT FROST

Too many people today only want to put in a forty-hour week. I always tell my managers that you can't be successful unless you tell your wife not to expect you home for dinner.
KEMMONS WILSON

Our greatest weariness comes from work not done.
ERIC HOFFER

Drive a nail home and clinch it so faithfully that you can wake up in the night and think of your work with satisfaction—a work at which you would not be ashamed to invoke the muse.
HENRY DAVID THOREAU

The reason why worry kills more people than work is that more people worry than work.
ROBERT FROST

Everything comes to him who hustles while he waits.
THOMAS EDISON

The average person puts only twenty-five percent of his energy and ability into his work. The world takes off its hat to those who put in more than fifty percent of their capacity, and stands on its head for those few and far between souls who devote one hundred percent.
ANDREW CARNEGIE

It is a commonplace observation that work expands to fill the time available for its completion.
C. NORTHCOTE PARKINSON

Labor disgraces no man; unfortunately you occasionally find men who disgrace labor.

ULYSSES S. GRANT

The brain is a wonderful organ; it starts working the moment you get up in the morning and doesn't stop until you get into the office.

ROBERT FROST

In the ordinary business of life, industry can do anything which genius can do, and very many things which it cannot.

HENRY WARD BEECHER

Don't bother about genius. Don't worry about being clever. Trust to hard work, perseverence, and determination. And the best motto for the long march is: "Don't grumble. Plug on!"

SIR FREDERICK TREVES

Most of life is routine—dull and grubby, but routine is the momentum that keeps a man going. If you wait for inspiration you'll be standing on the corner after the parade is a mile down the street.

BEN NICHOLAS

Concentration is my motto—first honesty, then industry, then concentration.

ANDREW CARNEGIE

What is work? A way to make a living? A way to keep busy? A glue to hold life together? Work is all these things and more. As an activity and as a symbol, work has always preoccupied us. We do it and we think about it. I go on working for the same reason that a hen goes on laying eggs.

H. L. MENCKEN

Perhaps it is this specter that most haunts working men and women: the planned obsolescence of people that is of a piece with the planned obsolescence of the things they make.

STUDS TERKEL

Employment, sir, and hardships, prevent melancholy.

SAMUEL JOHNSON

Punctuality is the soul of business.

THOMAS HALIBURTON

Punctuality is one of the cardinal business virtues: Always insist on it in your subordinates.

DON MARQUIS

Anyone can do any amount of work, provided it isn't the work he is *supposed* to be doing at that moment.

ROBERT BENCHLEY

One must work, if not from inclination, at least out of despair—since it proves on closest examination that work is less boring than amusing oneself.

CHARLES BAUDELAIRE

Wanting to work is so rare a want that it should be encouraged.

ABRAHAM LINCOLN

Men can do jointly what they cannot do singly; and the union of minds and hands, the concentration of their power, becomes almost omnipotent.

DANIEL WEBSTER

You will find men who want to be carried on the shoulders of others, who think that the world owes them a living. They don't seem to see that we must all lift together and pull together.

HENRY FORD

I am a friend of the working man, and I would rather be a friend than be one.

CLARENCE DARROW

I never knew a man escape failures, in either mind or body, who worked seven days a week.

SIR ROBERT PEEL

Those who work much do not work hard.
HENRY DAVID THOREAU

My rule always was to do the business of the day in the day.
DUKE OF WELLINGTON

There is more to life than increasing its speed.
MAHATMA GANDHI

Small opportunities are often the beginning of great enterprise.
DEMOSTHENES

There is hardly anything in the world that some men can't make a little worse and sell a little cheaper, and the people who consider price only are this man's lawful prey.
JOHN RUSKIN

Cheat me on the price but not on the goods.
THOMAS FULLER

The man who will use his skill and constructive imagination to see how much he can give for a dollar, instead of how little he give for a dollar, is bound to succeed.
HENRY FORD

I should never have made my success in life if I had not bestowed upon the least thing I have ever undertaken the same attention and care that I have bestowed upon the greatest.

CHARLES DICKENS

The only place where success comes before work is in the dictionary.

VIDAL SASSOON, *also attributed to* DONALD KENDALL

The will to succeed is important, but what's more important is the will to prepare.

BOBBY KNIGHT

What's money? A man is a success if he gets up in the morning and gets to bed at night, and in between he does what he wants to.

BOB DYLAN

All you need in this life is ignorance and confidence, and then success is sure.

MARK TWAIN

The successful businessman sometimes makes his money by ability and experience, but he generally makes it by mistake.

G. K. CHESTERTON

It is no wisdom ever to commend or discommend the actions of men by their success; for oftentimes some enterprises attempted by good counsel end unfortunately, and others inadvisedly taken in hand have happy success.

SIR WALTER RALEIGH

The best thing that can come with success is the knowledge that it is nothing to long for.

LIV ULLMANN

The success of each is dependent upon the success of the other.

JOHN D. ROCKEFELLER, JR.

It is not enough to succeed. Others must fail.

GORE VIDAL

The moral flabbiness born of the bitch-goddess SUCCESS. That—with the squalid interpretation put on the word success—is our national disease.

WILLIAM JAMES

The successful people are the ones who can think up stuff for the rest of the world to keep busy at.

DON MARQUIS

The toughest thing about success is that you've got to keep on being a success. Talent is only a starting point in business. You've go to keep working that talent.

IRVING BERLIN

My rise to the top was through sheer ability and inheritance.

MALCOLM FORBES

My formula for success? Rise early, work late, strike oil.

J. PAUL GETTY

If A equals success, then the formula is A equals X plus Y plus Z, with X being work, Y play, and Z keeping your mouth shut.

ALBERT EINSTEIN

Success usually comes to those who are too busy to be looking for it.

HENRY DAVID THOREAU

Suffer women once to arrive at an equality with you, and they will from that moment become your superiors.

CATO THE CENSOR

To be successful, a woman has to be much better at her job than a man.

GOLDA MEIR

A woman has to be twice as good as a man to go half as
far.

FANNIE HURST

Being a woman is a terribly difficult task, since it consists
principally in dealing with men.

JOSEPH CONRAD

Men always try to keep women out of business so they
won't find out how much fun it really is.

VIVIEN KELLEMS

Men are never so tired and harassed as when they deal
with a woman who wants a raise.

MICHAEL KORDA

Women will never be as successful as men because they
have no wives to advise them.

DICK VAN DYKE

Society is kinder to women who fail than to women who
succeed. Some men are, too.

SALLY QUINN

The man flaps about with a bunch of feathers; the woman
goes to work softly with a cloth.

OLIVER WENDELL HOLMES

If you want anything said, ask a man. If you want anything done, ask a woman.

MARGARET THATCHER

All women are ambitious naturally.

CHRISTOPHER MARLOWE

If women didn't exist, all the money in the world would have no meaning.

ARISTOTLE ONASSIS

Money and women. They're two of the strongest things in the world. The things you do for a woman you wouldn't do for anything else. Same with money.

SATCHEL PAIGE

If American men are obsessed with money, American women are obsessed with weight. The men talk of gain, the women talk of loss, and I do not know which talk is more boring.

MARYA MANNES

Power has no sex. Ambition and aggression are not masculine traits. Sensitivity and consensus-building are not female traits. Women must be willing to embrace all of these qualities—and use them to gain power.

KATHARINE GRAHAM

Power is the greatest aphrodisiac.
   HENRY A. KISSINGER

Power corrupts, but lack of power corrupts absolutely.
   ADLAI STEVENSON

Power tends to corrupt and absolute power corrupts absolutely.
   LORD ACTON

One of the first rules of playing the power game is that all bad news must be accepted calmly, as if one already knew and didn't care.
   MICHAEL KORDA

A friend in power is a friend lost.
   SAMUEL ADAMS

A man is to go about his business as if he had not a friend in the world to help him in it.
   LORD HALIFAX

A friendship founded on business is better than a business founded on friendship.
   JOHN D. ROCKEFELLER, JR.

Every successful enterprise requires three men—a dreamer, a businessman, and a son of a bitch.
   PETER MCARTHUR

My father always told me that all businessmen were sons of bitches, but I never believed it till now.

JOHN F. KENNEDY

I don't know the key to success, but the key to failure is trying to please everybody.

BILL COSBY

Nice guys finish last.

LEO DUROCHER

If people screw me, I screw back in spades.

DONALD TRUMP

I never give them hell. I give them the truth and they think it's hell.

HARRY TRUMAN

"Do other men, for they would do you." That's the true Business precept.

CHARLES DICKENS, *Martin Chuzzlewit*

No man lives without jostling and being jostled; in all ways he has to elbow himself through the world, giving and receiving offense.

PLAUTUS

When I pass a belt, I cannot resist hitting below it.
ROBERT MAXWELL, *also attributed to* MARGOT ASQUITH
on DAVID LLOYD GEORGE

I love to have enemies. I fight my enemies. I like beating my enemies to the ground.
DONALD TRUMP

If you want to make enemies, try to change something.
WOODROW WILSON

In the takeover business, if you want a friend, you buy a dog.
CARL ICAHN

Hostile corporate takeovers may be the most glaring example of organizing the firing squad in a circle. Hostile takeovers, as ends in themselves, typically combine zero productive enhancement with the redeeming social value of a feeding frenzy.
NORMAN AUGUSTINE

Takeover targets tend not to be badly run companies. If they were, raiders would have a harder time raising the money to buy them.
ANTHONY SOLOMON

Recently I learned that there are certain primitive tribes that practice *exocannibalism*, partaking of the flesh of their enemies only. Unfortunately, there are still some misguided groups, associations, and corporations that practice *endocannibalism* and only eat their friends.

GEORGE LANG

If you aren't fired with enthusiasm, you'll be fired with enthusiasm.

VINCE LOMBARDI

Can anybody remember when the times weren't hard and money not scarce?

RALPH WALDO EMERSON

When large numbers of men are unable to find work, unemployment results.

CALVIN COOLIDGE

It's a recession when your neighbor loses his job; it's a depression when you lose yours.

HARRY TRUMAN

If we face a recession, we should not lay off employees; the company should sacrifice a profit. It's management's risk and management's responsibility. Employees are not guilty; why should they suffer?

AKIO MORITA

64

If a business is unprofitable on account of bad management, want of enterprise, or out-worn methods, that is not a just reason for reducing the wages of its workers.

POPE PIUS XI

The biggest thing that has happened in the past decade is that no one feels secure. You can't cut forty percent of a company and have the sixty percent remaining assuming they have a job for life.

JAY CHIAT

The long-range solution to high unemployment is to increase the incentive of ordinary people to save, invest, work, and employ others. We make it costly for employers to employ people, and we subsidize people not to go to work. We have a system that increasingly taxes work and subsidizes nonwork.

MILTON FRIEDMAN

The taxpayer—that's someone who works for the federal government but doesn't have to take a civil service exam.

RONALD REAGAN

The art of taxation consists in so plucking the goose as to obtain the largest amount of feathers with the least amount of hissing.

JEAN BAPTISTE COLBERT

In general, the art of the government consists in taking as much money as possible from one party of the citizens to give to the other.

VOLTAIRE

After all, the chief business of the American people is business.

CALVIN COOLIDGE

The business of government is to keep the government out of business—that is, unless business needs government aid.

WILL ROGERS

Agriculture, manufactures, commerce, and navigation, the four pillars of our prosperity, are most thriving when left most to free enterprise.

THOMAS JEFFERSON

As soon as government management begins it upsets the natural equilibrium of industrial relations, and each interference only requires further bureaucratic control until the end is the tyranny of the totalitarian state.

ADAM SMITH *of Glasgow (1776)*

In all that the people can individually do well for themselves, government ought not to interfere.

ABRAHAM LINCOLN

The best minds are not in government. If any were, business would hire them away.

RONALD REAGAN

Christmas is a time when kids tell Santa what they want and adults pay for it. Deficits are when adults tell the government what they want—and their kids pay for it.

RICHARD LAMM

Blessed are the young, for they shall inherit the national debt.

HERBERT HOOVER

A national debt, if it is not excessive, will be to us a national blessing.

ALEXANDER HAMILTON

The only good budget is a balanced budget.

ADAM SMITH *of Glasgow (1776)*

The only good rule is that the budget should never be balanced—except for an instant when surplus to curb inflation is being altered to a deficit to fight deflation.

WARREN SMITH *of Ann Arbor (1965)*

No nation was ever ruined by trade.

BENJAMIN FRANKLIN

No nation was ever ruined on account of its debts.
ADOLF HITLER

Any government, like any family, can for a year spend a little more than it earns. But you and I know that a continuance of that habit means the poorhouse.
FRANKLIN DELANO ROOSEVELT

There is no art which one government sooner learns of another than that of draining money from the pockets of the people.
ADAM SMITH *of Glasgow (1776)*

There is no doubt that the real destroyer of the liberties of any people is he who spreads among them bounties, donations, and largess.
PLUTARCH

Inflation can be conquered by the continued application of public and private restraint, and by attention to long-run political policies that increase supply and productivity.
CHARLES SCHULTZE

Invest in inflation. It is the only thing going up.
WILL ROGERS

Inflation is the one form of taxation that can be imposed without legislation.

MILTON FRIEDMAN

We have a love-hate relationship. We hate inflation, but we love everything that causes it.

WILLIAM SIMON

A nickel ain't worth a dime anymore.

YOGI BERRA

The way to stop financial joyriding is to arrest the chauffeur, not the automobile.

WOODROW WILSON

Until you understand Capitalism you do not understand human society as it exists at present.

GEORGE BERNARD SHAW

I think that Capitalism, wisely managed, can probably be made more efficient for attaining economic ends than any alternate system yet in sight, but that in itself is in many ways extremely objectionable.

JOHN MAYNARD KEYNES

The power to tax . . . is not only the power to destroy but also the power to keep alive.

United States Supreme Court

The nation should have a tax system that looks like someone designed it on purpose.

WILLIAM SIMON

When there is an income tax, the just man will pay more and the unjust less on the same amount of income.

PLATO

Taxes are what we pay for a civilized society.

OLIVER WENDELL HOLMES, JR.

Unquestionably, there is progress. The average American now pays out almost as much in taxes alone, as he formerly got in wages.

H. L. MENCKEN

There is nothing sinister in so arranging one's affairs as to keep taxes as low as possible.

JUDGE LEARNED HAND

The hardest thing in the world to understand is the income tax.

ALBERT EINSTEIN

The income tax has made more liars out of the American people than gold has. Even when you make a tax form out on the level, you don't know, when it's through, if you are a crook or a martyr.

WILL ROGERS

From each according to his abilities, to each according to his needs.

KARL MARX

The entire graduated income tax structure was created by Karl Marx.

RONALD REAGAN

If you give Congress $1 of unnecessary taxes, they'll spend about $1.75 and that's inflationary. Inflation is un-American; therefore tax avoidance is patriotic.

WILLIAM DONOGHUE

Only little people pay taxes.

LEONA HELMSLEY, *allegedly said to her maid*

I have no use for bodyguards, but I have very special use for two highly trained certified public accountants.

ELVIS PRESLEY

Round numbers are always fake.

SAMUEL JOHNSON

There are two kinds of statistics, the kind you look up and the kind you make up.

REX STOUT

Never ask of money spent
Where the spender thinks it went.
Nobody was ever meant
To remember or invent
What he did with every cent.
ROBERT FROST

A little inaccuracy sometimes saves tons of explanation.
SAKI (H. H. MUNRO)

Economists are the great imperialists of the social sciences.
GARDNER ACKLEY

If ignorance paid dividends, most Americans could make a fortune out of what they don't know about economics.
LUTHER HODGES

The age of Chivalry is gone; that of sophistry, economists, and calculators has succeeded.
EDMUND BURKE

An economist is a man who states the obvious in terms of the incomprehensible.
ALFRED A. KNOPF

Booms and slumps are simply the expression of the results of an oscillation of the terms of credit about their equilibrium positions.

JOHN MAYNARD KEYNES

Just as war is too important to be left to the generals, so is an economic crisis too important to be left to the economists or "practical men."

JOHN KENNETH GALBRAITH

A man can be forgiven a lot if he can quote Shakespeare in an economic crisis.

PRINCE PHILLIP

If all the economists were laid end to end, they'd never reach a conclusion.

GEORGE BERNARD SHAW

The instability of the economy is equaled only by the instability of the economists.

JOHN H. WILLIAMS

I am now a Keynesian.

RICHARD NIXON

We are all Keynesians now.

JOHN MAYNARD KEYNES

Whenever there are great strains or changes in the economic system, it tends to generate crackpot theories which then find their way into the legislative channels.

DAVID STOCKMAN

There is no sadder sight in the world than to see a beautiful theory killed by a brutal fact.

THOMAS HUXLEY

You cannot run a business, or anything else, on theory.

HAROLD GENEEN

The volume of paper expands to fill the available briefcases.

GOVERNOR JERRY BROWN

If you don't know what to do with many of the papers piled on your desk, stick a dozen colleagues' initials on 'em, and pass them along. When in doubt, route.

MALCOLM FORBES

If your desk isn't cluttered, you probably aren't doing your job.

HAROLD GENEEN

Keep things informal. Talking is a natural way to do business. Writing is great for keeping records and putting down details, but talk generates ideas. Great things come from our luncheon meetings which consist of a sandwich, a cup of soup, and a good idea or two. No martinis.

T. BOONE PICKENS

Never meet anybody after two for lunch. Meet in the morning because you are sharper. Never have long lunches. They're not only boring, but dangerous because of the martinis.

JOSEPH P. KENNEDY

If figures of speech based on sport and fornication were suddenly banned, American corporate communication would be reduced to pure mathematics.

JAY MCINERNEY, *Brightness Falls*

If you don't have anything to say, sing it.

ADVERTISING SAYING, QUOTED BY DAVID OGILVY

Advertising is a valuable economic factor because it is the cheapest way of selling goods, especially if the goods are worthless.

SINCLAIR LEWIS

Advertising is like learning—a little is a dangerous thing.

P. T. BARNUM

There are three things that every man can do better than anyone else. One is coach a football team. The second is judge a beauty contest. The third is write advertising.
BERT SUGAR

Advertisements contain the only truths to be relied on in a newspaper.
THOMAS JEFFERSON

Promise, large promise, is the soul of an advertisement.
SAMUEL JOHNSON

Advertising is the modern substitute for argument; its function is to make the worse appear better.
GEORGE SANTAYANA

You can tell the ideals of a nation by its advertisements.
NORMAN DOUGLAS

You can fool all of the people all of the time if the advertising is right and the budget is big enough.
JOSEPH E. LEVINE

Advertising is eighty-five percent confusion and fifteen percent commission.
FRED ALLEN

The guy you've really got to reach with your advertising
is the copywriter for your chief rival's advertising agency.
If you can terrorize him, you've got it licked.

HOWARD L. GOSSAGE

The codfish lays 10,000 eggs,
The homely hen just one;
The codfish never cackles
To tell you that she's done.
And so we scorn the codfish,
And the homely hen we prize.
Which demonstrates to you and me
That it pays to advertise.

The Toronto Globe

When the client moans and sighs
Make his logo twice the size.
If he still should prove refractory,
Show a picture of his factory.
Only in the gravest cases
Should you show the clients' faces.

ANONYMOUS

Nothing except the mint can make money without advertising.

THOMAS B. MACAULAY

Anything you do to enhance sales is a promotion.
BILL VEECK

I play to people's fantasies. People may not always think big themselves, but they can still get very excited by those who do. That's why a little hyperbole never hurts. . . . I call it truthful hyperbole.
DONALD TRUMP

The first Rotarian was the first man to call John the Baptist, Jack.
H. L. MENCKEN

The meek have to inherit the earth—they sure don't know how to market it.
JENO PALUCCI

Emerson said that if you build a better mousetrap the world will beat a path to your door, and that may have been true then . . . but it's not true now. No one will come. You have to package and promote that mousetrap. Then they will come.
CHARLES GILLETTE

Anonymous marketing just doesn't work anymore. Consumers want to know not only *what* they are buying, but *who* they're buying it from. The people, not the *logo*. Consumer relations development is as important as the product itself.

FRANK PERDUE

The craft of the merchant is this, bringing a thing from where it abounds to where it is costly.

RALPH WALDO EMERSON

It is well-known what a middleman is: He is a man who bamboozles one party and plunders the other.

BENJAMIN DISRAELI

The by-product is sometimes more valuable than the product.

HAVELOCK ELLIS

Buy something people use and throw away.

BERNARD BARUCH

Paying attention to simple little things that most men neglect makes a few men rich.

HENRY FORD

Only a fool holds out for the top dollar.

JOSEPH P. KENNEDY

Buying is cheaper than asking.
  German proverb

If I had to live my life over again, I would elect to be a trader of goods rather than a student of science. I think barter is a noble thing.
  ALBERT EINSTEIN

Rule 1. The customer is always right.
Rule 2. If the customer is ever wrong, reread Rule 1.
  STEW LEONARD

There is only one boss. The customer. And he can fire everybody in the company, from the chairman on down, simply by spending his money somewhere else.
  SAM WALTON

Any fool can paint a picture, but it takes a wise man to be able to sell it.
  SAMUEL BUTLER

There is more similarity in the marketing challenge of selling a precious painting by Degas and a frosted mug of root beer than you ever thought possible.
  ALFRED TAUBMAN, *owner of Sotheby's*

Being good in business is the most fascinating kind of art.
  ANDY WARHOL

It is a great art to know how to sell wind.
BALTASAR GRACIÁN

Don't try to explain it; just sell it.
COLONEL TOM PARKER

To sell something, tell a woman it's a bargain; tell a man it's deductible.
EARL WILSON

People will buy anything that's one to a customer.
SINCLAIR LEWIS

And for a salesman there is no rock bottom to the life. He don't put a bolt to a nut, he don't tell you the law or give you medicine. He's a man 'way out there in the blue, riding on a smile and a shoeshine. And when they start not smiling back—that's an earthquake.
ARTHUR MILLER, *Death of a Salesman*

Everyone lives by selling something.
ROBERT LOUIS STEVENSON

To lead the people, walk behind them.
LAO-TZU

Leadership appears to be the act of getting others to want to do something you are convinced should be done.
VANCE PACKARD

You don't have to be intellectually bright to be a leader.
SIR EDMUND HILLARY

Good management consists in showing *average* people how to do the work of *superior* people.
JOHN D. ROCKEFELLER, JR.

There are times when even the best manager is like the little boy with the big dog waiting to see where the dog wants to go so he can take him there.
LEE IACOCCA

The secret of managing is to keep the five guys who hate you away from the five who are undecided.
CASEY STENGEL

Managing is like holding a dove in your hand. Squeeze too hard and you kill it; not hard enough and it flies away.
TOMMY LASORDA

Eagles don't flock—you've got to find them one at a time.
H. ROSS PEROT

When you soar like an eagle, you attract the hunters.
MILTON S. GOULD

The question, "Who ought to be boss?" is like asking, "Who ought to be tenor in the quartet?" Obviously, the man who can sing tenor.

HENRY FORD

The big salaries in business always go to those who have what it takes to get things done. That is true not only of those executives who guide the destinies of a business, but it is true of those upon whom executives must depend for results.

J. C. ASPLEY

Businessmen tend to grow old early. They are committed to security and stability. They won't rock the boat and won't gamble, denying the future for a nearsighted present. They forget what made them successful in the first place.

PETER GOLDMARK

It is the nature of a man as he grows older to protest against change, particularly change for the better.

JOHN STEINBECK

The man who builds a factory builds a temple; the man who works there worships there; and to each is due not scorn and blame but reverence and praise.

CALVIN COOLIDGE

Nothing is more difficult, and therefore more precious, than to be able to decide.

NAPOLEON BONAPARTE

If I had to sum up in one word what makes a good manager, I'd say decisiveness. You can use the fanciest computers to gather the numbers, but in the end you have to set a timetable and *act*.

LEE IACOCCA

Be willing to make decisions. That's the most important quality in a good leader. Don't fall victim to what I call the "ready-aim-aim-aim syndrome." You must be willing to fire.

T. BOONE PICKENS

If I made a decision fast, I was right sixty percent of the time. If I made a decision carefully, I'd be right seventy percent, but it was always worth it.

EDMUND C. LYNCH

Executive ability is deciding quickly and getting someone else to do the work.

J. G. POLLARD

A man who has to be convinced to act before he acts is *not* a man of action.

GEORGES CLEMENCEAU

86

Success tends to go not to the person who is error-free, because he also tends to be risk-averse. Rather it goes to the person who recognizes that life is pretty much a percentage business. It isn't making mistakes that's critical; it's correcting them and getting on with the principal task.

DONALD RUMSFELD

A chief is a man who assumes responsibility. He says, "I was beaten," he does not say, "My men were beaten."

ANTOINE DE SAINT-EXUPÉRY

If anything goes bad, I did it.
If anything goes semi-good, then we did it.
If anything goes real good, then you did it.
That's all it takes to get people to win football games.

PAUL "BEAR" BRYANT

A man isn't a man until he has to meet a payroll.

IVAN SHAFFER

To be a manager, you have to start at the bottom—no exceptions.

HENRY BLOCK

Never tell people how to do things. Tell them what to do and they will surprise you with their ingenuity.

GENERAL GEORGE PATTON

The surest way for an executive to kill himself is to refuse to learn how and when and to whom to delegate.

J. C. PENNEY

I have an absolute rule. I refuse to make a decision that somebody else can make. The first rule of leadership is to save yourself for the big decision. Don't allow your mind to become cluttered with the trivia. Don't let yourself become the issue.

RICHARD NIXON

The perfect bureaucrat everywhere is the man who manages to make no decisions and escape all responsibility.

BROOKS ATKINSON

Guidelines for Bureaucrats:
(1) When in charge, ponder.
(2) When in trouble, delegate.
(3) When in doubt, mumble.

JAMES H. BOREN

Be a yardstick of quality. Some people aren't used to an environment where excellence is expected.

STEPHEN JOBS

A real executive goes around with a worried look on his assistants' faces.

VINCE LOMBARDI

The Executive is
A busy man
Who sits around
On his frustrated can.
FRED ALLEN

A mean streak is a very important quality of leadership.
CHARLES GOODELL

Good fellows are a dime a dozen, but an aggressive leader is priceless.
EARL "RED" BLAIK

You can get more with a kind word and a gun, than you can with a kind word.
AL CAPONE

Make every decision as if you owned the company.
ROBERT TOWNSEND

Patience is a most necessary quality for business: Many a man would rather you heard his story than granted his request.
EARL OF CHESTERFIELD

Most of the successful people I've known are ones who do more listening than talking. If you choose your company carefully, it's worth listening to what they have to say.

You don't have to blow out the other fellow's light to let your own shine.

BERNARD BARUCH

Frustration is your worst enemy. You have to continue to stop yourself from letting frustration drive you to make irrational decisions—or rely on your advisors to stop you. When we put a deal together, I have the ability to focus on exactly what we're working on and close out everything else.

HENRY KRAVIS

Efficiency is doing things right. Effectiveness is doing the right thing.

ZIG ZIGLAR

Never leave well-enough alone.

RAYMOND LOEWY

When you get right down to it, one of the most important tasks of a manager is to eliminate his people's excuse for failure.

ROBERT TOWNSEND

It is no use saying, "We are doing our best." You have got to succeed in doing what is necessary.

WINSTON CHURCHILL

Failures are like skinned knees—painful, but superficial.
H. ROSS PEROT

Never give up a man until he has failed at something he likes.
LEWIS E. LAWES

Big shots are only little shots who keep shooting.
CHRISTOPHER MORLEY

At too many companies, the boss shoots the arrow of managerial performance and then hastily paints the bull's-eye around the spot where it lands.
WARREN BUFFETT

People are known as much by the quality of their failures as by the quality of their successes.
MARK MCCORMACK

Good people are good because they've come to wisdom through failure. We get very little wisdom from success, you know.
WILLIAM SAROYAN

What made me a success in business would make me a failure as a politician.
H. ROSS PEROT

I find it rather easy to portray a businessman. Being bland, rather cruel, and incompetent comes naturally to me.

JOHN CLEESE

Never be a pioneer; it doesn't pay. Let the other man do the pioneering and then after he has shown what can be done, do it bigger and more quickly; but let the other man take the time and risk to show you how to do it.

LEO BAKELAND

Few great men could pass Personnel.

PAUL GOODMAN

Entrepreneurship is the last refuge of the troublemaking individual.

JAMES K. GLASSMAN

The entrepreneur, especially when starting out, knows that he is operating on the threshold of success or failure. A single mistake can ruin him.

HAROLD GENEEN

When you can do the common things of life in an uncommon way, you will command the attention of the world.

GEORGE WASHINGTON CARVER

Throughout my career, the things I've done best are the things people told me couldn't be done.

H. ROSS PEROT

No one can possibly achieve any real and lasting success or get rich in business by being a conformist.
J. PAUL GETTY

It is better to fail in originality than to succeed in imitation.
HERMAN MELVILLE

If you can't imitate him, don't copy him.
YOGI BERRA

A hunch is creativity trying to tell you something.
FRANK CAPRA

I do much of my creative thinking while golfing. If people know you are working at home they think nothing of walking in for a coffee. But they wouldn't dream of interrupting you on the golf course.
HARPER LEE

Serious-minded people have few ideas. People with ideas are never serious.
PAUL VALÉRY

I probably have traveled and walked into more variety stores than anybody in America. I am just trying to get ideas, any kind of ideas that will help our company. Most of us don't invent ideas. We take the best ideas from someone else.
SAM WALTON

If economists were any good at business, they would be rich men instead of advisers to rich men.

KIRK KERKORIAN

Please find me a one-armed economist so we will not always hear, "On the other hand. . . ."

HERBERT HOOVER

Even children learn in growing up that "both" is not an admissable answer to the choice "which one."

PAUL SAMUELSON

We have become to some extent, I think, economic hypochondriacs. You get a wiggle in a statistic . . . and everyone runs to get a thermometer.

PAUL MCCRACKEN

I think there are two areas where new ideas are terribly dangerous—economics and sex. By and large, it's all been tried before, and if it's new, it's probably illegal or unhealthy.

FELIX ROHATYN

There are no new forms of financial fraud; in the last hundred years there have only been small variations of a few classic designs.

JOHN KENNETH GALBRAITH

Experts should be on tap but never on top.
WINSTON CHURCHILL

Committee—a group of men who keep minutes and waste hours.
MILTON BERLE

Nothing is ever accomplished by committee unless it consists of three members, one of whom happens to be sick and the other absent.
HENDRIK VAN LOON

Parkinson's Law of Triviality: The time spent on any item of the agenda will be in inverse proportion to the sum involved.
C. NORTHCOTE PARKINSON

You know, if an orange and an apple went into conference consultations, it might come out a pear.
RONALD REAGAN

Having served on various committees I have drawn up a
    list of rules:
    Never arrive on time; this stamps you as a beginner.
    Don't say anything until the meeting is half over; this
        stamps you as wise.
    Be as vague as possible; this avoids irritating the others.
    When in doubt, suggest a subcommittee be appointed.

Be the first to move for adjournment; this will make you popular; it's what everyone is waiting for.
HARRY CHAPMAN

Outside of traffic, there is nothing that has held this country back as much as committees.
WILL ROGERS

The reason that everybody likes planning is that nobody has to do anything.
GOVERNOR JERRY BROWN

I can give you a six-word formula for success, Think things through—then follow through.
EDDIE RICKENBACKER

Strategic planning is worthless—unless there is first a strategic vision.
JOHN NAISBITT

Consultant: any ordinary guy more than fifty miles from home.
ERIC SEVAREID

Make three correct guesses consecutively and you will establish a reputation as an expert.
LAURENCE PETER

Management consultants are people who borrow your watch to tell you what time it is, and then walk off with it.
ROBERT TOWNSEND

The real problem is what to do with the problem solvers after the problems are solved.
GAY TALESE

Problems are the price of progress. Don't bring me anything but trouble. Good news weakens me.
CHARLES F. KETTERING

In a difficult business, no sooner is one problem solved than another surfaces—never is there just one cockroach in the kitchen.
WARREN BUFFETT

Problems are only opportunities in work clothes.
HENRY KAISER

Opportunities are usually disguised as hard work, so most people don't recognize them.
ANN LANDERS

A problem well stated is a problem half solved.
CHARLES F. KETTERING

To err is human but to really foul up requires a computer.
PAUL ERLICH

Computers are useless. They can only give you answers.
PABLO PICASSO

One machine can do the work of fifty ordinary men. No machine can do the work of one extraordinary man.
ELBERT HUBBARD

A computer does not substitute for judgment anymore than a pencil substitutes for literacy. But writing without a pencil is no particular advantage.
ROBERT MCNAMARA

We've got to make sure we don't create organizations with a CEO at the top, a computer in the middle, and lots of workers at the bottom.
ROBERT T. TOMASKO

Technological progress has merely provided us with more efficient means for going backwards.
ALDOUS HUXLEY

What's going to happen to the executive's job in the next ten years? Nothing. It is amazing how many jobs are exactly the same as they were in 1900.
PETER DRUCKER

Most employers these days are more interested in performance than conformance.

HENRY FORD II

A 10,000-aspirin job.
Japanese term for executive responsibility

America is the country where you buy a lifetime supply
of aspirin for one dollar, and use it up in two weeks.

JOHN BARRYMORE

Fortunately for us, Japan is opening its first business
school in the near future. This is likely to produce a
measurable drop in Japanese productivity.

FELIX ROHATYN

The secret of Japanese success is not technology, but a
special way of managing people—a style that focuses a
strong company philosophy, a distinct corporate culture,
long-range staff development, and consensus decision
making.

WILLIAM OUCHI

Hitch your wagon to a star.

RALPH WALDO EMERSON

The best executive is the one who has sense enough to pick good men to do what he wants done, and self-restraint enough to keep from meddling with them while they do it.

THEODORE ROOSEVELT

The most successful highest-up executives carefully select understudies. They don't strive to do everything themselves. They train and trust others. This leaves them foot-free, mind-free, with time to think. They have time to receive important callers, to pay worthwhile visits. They have time for their families. No matter how able, any employer or executive who insists on running a one-man enterprise courts unhappy circumstances when his powers dwindle.

B. C. FORBES

I am always looking for people who can do a job better than I can.

T. BOONE PICKENS

Hire people who are smarter than you are.

LEW WASSERMAN

Never hire your client's children.

DAVID OGILVY

I made myself almost too good as Number Two. So, in effect, what I had to do to get promoted was to get my boss promoted. Which I would advise anyone. That may

sound cynical, but if you want to get ahead, promote
your boss.

WILLIAM GEORGE

If you get to be thirty-five and your job still involves
wearing a name tag, you've probably made a serious voca-
tional error.

DENNIS MILLER

The first-rate man will try to surround himself with his
equals, or betters if possible. The second-rate man will
surround himself with third-rate men. The third-rate
man will surround himself with fifth-rate men.

ANDRÉ WEIL

In a hierarchy, every employee tends to rise to his level
of incompetence.

LAURENCE PETER

To blame a promotion that fails on the promoted person,
as is usually done, is no more rational than to blame a
capital investment that has gone sour on the money that
was put into it.

PETER DRUCKER

The employer generally gets the employees he deserves.

SIR WALTER BILBEY

Be awful nice to 'em going up, because you're going to meet 'em coming down.
JIMMY DURANTE

The man who makes an appearance in the business world, the man who creates personal interest, is the man who gets ahead. Be liked and you will never want.
ARTHUR MILLER

The ability to deal with people is as purchasable a commodity as sugar or coffee. And I pay more for that ability than for any other under the sun.
JOHN D. ROCKEFELLER, JR.

The greatest ability in business is to get along with others and influence their actions. A chip on the shoulder is too heavy a piece of baggage to carry through life.
JOHN HANCOCK

When two men in business always agree, one of them is unnecessary.
WILLIAM WRIGLEY, JR.

It were not best that we should all think alike; it is difference of opinion that makes horse races.
MARK TWAIN

Difference of opinion leads to inquiry, and inquiry leads to truth.

THOMAS JEFFERSON

When you say that you agree to a thing in principle you mean that you have not the slightest intention of carrying it out in practice.

BISMARCK

When people agree with me, I always feel that I must be wrong.

OSCAR WILDE

Echo men are very important in the field of advertising. They are men who follow in the wake of the big executive and echo his sentiments as they are expressed.

FRED ALLEN

I don't want any yes-men around me. I want everyone to tell the truth—even though it costs him his job.

SAMUEL GOLDWYN

Always mistrust a subordinate who never finds fault with his superior.

JOHN CHURTON COLLINS

Capitalize upon criticism. It's one of the hardest things in the world to accept criticism, especially when it's not presented in a constructive way, and turn it to your advantage.

J. C. PENNEY

I have heard your views. They do not harmonize with mine. The decision is taken unanimously.

CHARLES DE GAULLE

The only way to get the best of an argument is to avoid it.

DALE CARNEGIE

When I am getting ready to reason with a man I spend one-third of my time thinking about myself and what I am going to say, and two-thirds thinking about him and what he is going to say.

ABRAHAM LINCOLN

Whenever you're sitting across from some important person, always picture him sitting in a suit of long underwear. That's the way I always operated in business.

JOSEPH P. KENNEDY

I find it helpful to try to figure out in advance where the other person would like to end up—at what point he will do the deal and still feel like he's coming away with something. This is different from "How far will he go?"

A lot of times you can push someone to the wall, and you still reach an agreement, but his resentment will come back to haunt you in a million ways.

MARK McCORMACK

My style of dealmaking is quite simple and straightforward. I just keep pushing and pushing and pushing to get what I'm after.

DONALD TRUMP

Many promising reconciliations have broken down because, while both parties came prepared to forgive, neither party came prepared to be forgiven.

CHARLES WILLIAMS

If you can't convince 'em, confuse 'em.

HARRY TRUMAN

A criminal is a person with predatory instincts who has not sufficient capital to form a corporation.

ROBERT W. KENT

A corporation is an artificial being, invisible, intangible, and existing only in contemplation of law.

JOHN MARSHALL

Corporation: an ingenious device for obtaining individual profit without individual responsibility.

AMBROSE BIERCE

Corporations are invisible, immortal, and have no soul.
ascribed to ROGER MANWOOD, *chief baron of the English Exchequer, 1592*

Corporations . . . are many lesser commonwealths in the bowels of a greater, like worms in the entrails of a natural man.
THOMAS HOBBES

Capitalists are no more capable of self-sacrifice than a man is capable of lifting himself by his own bootstraps.
LENIN

What is good for the country is good for General Motors, and what is good for General Motors is good for the country.
CHARLES E. WILSON

A big corporation is more or less blamed for being big; it is only big because it gives service. If it doesn't give service, it gets small faster than it grew big.
WILLIAM KNUDSEN

I spent my youth worrying about corporate power. Now I worry about corporate incompetence.
JOHN KENNETH GALBRAITH

Big Business is basic to the very life of this country; and yet many—perhaps most—Americans have a deep-seated fear and an emotional repugnance to it. Here is monumental contradiction.

DAVID LILIENTHAL

Big Business is not dangerous because it is big, but because its bigness is an unwholesome inflation created by privilege and exemptions which it ought not to enjoy.

WOODROW WILSON

There's a perception in this country that you're better off if you're in two lousy businesses than if you're in one good one.

ROBERT C. GOIZETTA

One cannot walk through a mass-production factory and not feel that one is in hell.

W. H. AUDEN

One way to avoid having industrial troubles is to avoid having industries.

DON MARQUIS

Retirement at sixty-five is ridiculous. When I was sixty-five I still had pimples.

GEORGE BURNS

When a man retires, his wife gets twice the husband, but only half the income.
CHI CHI RODRIGUEZ

Retirement kills more people than hard work ever did.
MALCOLM FORBES

He's no failure. He's not dead yet.
WILLIAM LLOYD GEORGE

The man who dies rich, dies disgraced.
ANDREW CARNEGIE

There is a great deal of truth in Andrew Carnegie's remark, "The man who dies rich, dies disgraced." I should add, the man who lives rich, lives disgraced.
AGA KHAN III

I have the feeling that in a balanced life one should die penniless. The trick is dismantling.
ART GARFUNKEL

You can be young without money, but you can't be old without it.
ELIZABETH TAYLOR, *Cat on a Hot Tin Roof*

When I was young I thought that money was the most important thing in life; now that I am old, I know it is.
OSCAR WILDE

When you have told anyone you have left him a legacy, the only decent thing to do is die at once.
SAMUEL BUTLER

There's no reason to be the richest man in the cemetery. You can't do any business from there.
COLONEL SANDERS

When I die, my epitaph should read: *She Paid the Bills*. That's the story of my private life.
GLORIA SWANSON

There are worse things in life than death. Have you ever spent an evening with an insurance salesman?
WOODY ALLEN

My work is done. Why wait?
GEORGE EASTMAN, *founder of Kodak, in his suicide note*

I am guardedly optimistic about the next world, but remain cognizant of the downside risks.
JEREMY GLUCK's *prediction of what* ALLAN GREENSPAN's *epitaph will read*

The bottom line is in heaven.
EDWIN LAND

INDEX

Rockefeller, David, 10
Rockefeller, John D. Jr., 2,
  32, 56, 61, 84, 104
Rockne, Knute, 4
Rodriguez, Chi Chi, 111
Rogers, Will, 36, 41, 44, 66,
  69, 71, 97
Rohatyn, Felix, 95, 100
Rooney, Andy, 23
Roosevelt, Franklin Delano,
  69
Roosevelt, Theodore, 34, 42,
  102
Rose, Billy, 32
Rothstein, Arnold, 17
Rumsfeld, Donald, 87
Runyon, Damon, 17, 35
Ruskin, John, 54
Russell, Bertrand, 25

Sadat, Anwar, 25
Saki (H. H. Munro), 29, 73
Samuelson, Paul, 95
Sanders, Colonel, 112
Santayana, George, 77
Sarnoff, David, 11
Sarnoff, Robert, 30
Saroyan, William, 92
Sarton, May, 18
Sassoon, Vidal, 55
Schultze, Charles, 69
Schwartzkopf, Norman, 6
Seneca, 36

Sevareid, Eric, 97
Shaffer, Ivan, 87
Shakespeare, William, 35, 40
Shaw, Goerge Bernard, 12,
  70, 74
Sherrod, William "Blackie,"
  34
Sign (retail stores), 30
Simon, Neil, 13, 22
Simon, William, 70, 71
Smith, Adam, 66, 67, 69
Smith, Logan Pearsall, 22,
  27
Smith, Warren, 67
Snead, Sam, 4
Solomon, Anthony, 63
Stein, Gertrude, 15, 27
Steinbeck, John, 85
Steinmetz, Charles, 22, 47
Stengel, Casey, 84
Stevenson, Adlai, 61
Stevenson, Robert Louis, 83
Stockman, David, 75
Stout, Rex, 72
Sugar, Bert, 77
Sutton, Don, 41
Sutton, Willie, 37
Swanson, Gloria, 112

Talese, Gay, 88
Taubman, Alfred, 82
Taylor, Elizabeth, 111
Terkel, Studs, 52